HISTORY
of the
SPIRIT LAKE MASSACRE!
[IOWA, 1857]
and of
MISS ABIGAIL GARDINER'S
THREE MONTHS' CAPTIVITY
AMONG THE INDIANS
ACCORDING TO HER OWN ACCOUNT

Lorenzo Porter Lee

HERITAGE BOOKS
2011

HERITAGE BOOKS
AN IMPRINT OF HERITAGE BOOKS, INC.

Books, CDs, and more—Worldwide

For our listing of thousands of titles see our website
at
www.HeritageBooks.com

A Facsimile Reprint
Published 2011 by
HERITAGE BOOKS, INC.
Publishing Division
100 Railroad Ave. #104
Westminster, Maryland 21157

Entered according to Act of Congress
in the year 1857, by L. P. Lee
in the Clerk's Office of the District Court of Connecticut

— Publisher's Notice —
In reprints such as this, it is often not possible to remove blemishes from the original. We feel the contents of this book warrant its reissue despite these blemishes and hope you will agree and read it with pleasure.

International Standard Book Numbers
Paperbound: 978-0-7884-3405-1
Clothbound: 978-0-7884-8796-5

CONTENTS.

		PAGE.
PREFACE,		3
CHAP. I.	INTRODUCTION,	5
CHAP. II.	MR. GARDINER AT SENECA,	7
CHAP. III.	SPIRIT LAKE,	9
CHAP. IV.	INDIANS,	13
CHAP. V.	MASSACRE,	15
CHAP. VI.	THE CAPTIVES BEGIN THE MARCH,	19
CHAP. VII.	THE JOURNEY,	20
CHAP. VIII.	DROWNING AND SHOOTING OF MRS. THATCHER,	24
CHAP. IX.	MRS. NOBLE'S FATE,	26
CHAP. X.	INTERESTING DETAILS,	28
CHAP. XI.	BURIAL OF VICTIMS,	31
CHAP. XII.	EFFORTS MADE TO RESCUE THE CAPTIVES,—MISS GARDINER'S RETURN,	33
CHAP. XIII.	PLEASANT TRAVEL,—MISS GARDINER,	43
CHAP. XIV.	RETRIBUTION,—DEATH,—MALEDICTION,	45

PREFACE.

This thrilling tale of suffering and wrong, is written for a double purpose. That its readers in the older and more settled States may the better appreciate the blessings of Peace and Civilization when contrasted with the dangers and privations of Pioneer Life, and that a young and bereaved survivor of a murdered family may be profited by its circulation.

PRESS OF CASE, LOCKWOOD AND COMPANY.

INTRODUCTION. 5

From a Daguerreotype taken at St. Pauls, June 23, 1857.

CHAPTER I.

"No radiant pearl which crested Fortune wears,
No gem that twinkling hangs from Beauty's ears;
Not the bright stars which Night's blue arch adorn;
No rising sun that gilds the vernal morn;
Shine with such lustre as the tear that flows
Down virtue's manly cheek for others woes."—*Darwin.*

IT is no easy matter for us who have never seen death in his most savage forms, never lived in scenes of bloodshed, never suffered from privation and want, never braved the rough-and-tumble life of the prairie, or dared the war-whoop and scalping-knife, to realize fully the horrors described in the following pages. Had they transpired in New York or any of our more populous cities, they would have kindled the sympathies of the whole nation, and excited a world-wide interest. The daily papers would have trebled their circulation while magnifying every incident connected with the "Horrible Tragedy." Every act, every word, every look of the savage perpetrators of such outrages, would be reported to thousands of eager readers. Social circles would for weeks, talk or think of nothing else. The streets, the hotels, the saloons, the thoroughfares of business, the steamboats, rail-cars, and in short, every resort of the living, would ring with the interesting gossip relating to the barbarous massacre. Miss Abigail Gardiner would become a heroine of the most enviable notoriety. Throngs would press to behold her expressive face; crowds would be anxious to know every word that might escape from her lips for months, and she, with all her relatives and fellow-sufferers, would at once take rank among the historical characters of the age. Human hearts vibrate most with sympathy when near the exciting cause, but like the gently rippling waters far off from the falling stone, they are very slightly moved by the troubles of those at a distance.

Accordingly, we at the east have felt, comparatively, but little sympathy in the Spirit Lake Massacre, while wrath and sympathy have lashed the hearts of our Western countrymen with a tempest of excitement, the surging swells of which are still heard moaning their solemn dirge. Who that gazes upon Miss Gardiner's well formed features, sees the depth of her eyes, the character and strength of endurance and of self-command, and yet the almost enslaved submissiveness, the despairing indifference to fate, the keen suffering and grief, all stamped on her countenance, and shaded by the tawn of her ruthless captors, can read the soul-harrowing tale of her tortures, without a tear of sympathy for the afflicted maiden, and an unutterable feeling of indignation against her foul tormentors?

As children, we have all read with exciting interest, the story of the attacks of the Indians on the early settlers of our country. We have felt for the distracted family of Mr. Williams, of Deerfield, Mass., execrated the barbarities committed by the Indians upon Saratoga, and upon the early settlers in Virginia, wept over the bloody murder of Miss McCrea, the luckless victims of Wyoming, and followed with tears and admiration the fortunes of Daniel Boone and his brave companions in Kentucky, but we doubt whether among all these, bloodier tomahawks ever gleamed, than those which hewed down the settlers at Spirit Lake, or greater fortitude was ever exhibited than that which so heroically shines in Miss ABIGAIL GARDINER.

CHAPTER II.

"What's his name and birth?"—SHAK., *Cym.*, Act 1, *Sc.* 1.

In Seneca, N. Y., might have been seen some years ago, on the bank of a rapid and picturesqe stream, a modest but substantial factory. In this building it was, that Mr. Roland Gardiner patiently toiled for many years in making combs. Mr. Gardiner was a member of the Methodist church, as was also his worthy wife, and during their stay in Seneca, were strong supporters and consistent ornaments in the communion of their choice. Their marriage was blessed by the birth of four children. Mary was the eldest, Eliza Matilda the second, Abigail, (who is the heroine of this faithful history,) the third, and Rowland, the youngest and the only son. Alas that Abigail and Eliza should now be the sole survivors of this once happy circle!

While laboring at his combs in the factory, Mr. Gardiner, encouraged and assisted by the judicious frugality and cheerful industry of his excellent wife, succeeded in raising his fortune to the comfortable little sum (in those days,) of three thousand dollars. Perhaps if content with such slow but sure gains, he had remained until now in his former residence and vocation, death would not yet have cut off him and his family, but they might have amassed a snug fortune, and been living in ease and comfort. The war-whoop of the Indian would never have echoed through his peaceful cottage, the scalping knife never would have horrified his children and sent them and their beloved parents to an untimely grave in the wilderness, nor would this history ever have been called for. But as "man never is, but always to be blessed;" no doubt Mr. Gardiner, like the rest of his race, felt sure that he might do better elsewhere. Perhaps, touched with the Western Fever, which has become the chronic epidemic of the Anglo Saxon race, and indeed of nearly all Europe; perhaps impelled by the love of change, (which is now the characteristic of Americans no less than of the French,) or, it may be, for some nobler and better reason than any of these, Mr. Gardiner gave up his factory and well-furnished dwelling in New York, and with his young and interesting family, began the world anew in the State of Ohio. It was in the year 1852, when the first cool winds of Autumn had chilled the glows of Summer life, when the grass was changing to a paler green, and all vegetation was mottled by the bright hectic flushes of approaching Fall, and nature seemed to sympathize with the departing family, that Mr. Gardiner, with all that he owned and held dearest on earth, sadly bade adieu to the scenes of many happy and prosperous years. The stirring bustle of his factory, with its whizzing wheels, and the merry clink-clank of its machinery had to be given up. The refreshing and familiar rushing of his water-fall, with all the lively and accustomed associations that hovered around it, were exchanged for the broad, rich western prairie, and the new and more exciting adventures of pioneer life. The long, heavy canvas-covered emigrant wagon, after a tedious journey, brought its passengers to Edyington, Ohio, where Mr. Gardiner and his family engaged in keeping a boarding-house.

But as the leaves which were falling around him at the time of his departure from his home, are, when broken from the stem, the more easily whirled away by the first breeze that puffs them, so Mr. Gardiner found it very easy and natural, when once having begun to move, to pull up stakes again, and seek his fortune still further West. His experience, is that of thousands of us Americans. We seem to believe that because it may seem good for some to "go West," it is best for each one of us to go farthest West of all, and so we keep running a continual race, and chase the setting sun, as if, like the boy in pursuit of the end of the rainbow, we were sure of finding a pot of gold at our journey's end. In this, however, we are but obeying an evident decree of Providence. The posterity of Japhet, who is our Great-Grand Father, will to the end of time, prove the truth of the prophecy, "*God shall enlarge Japhet, and he shall dwell in the tents of Shem.*" In obedience then, to the general custom of his countrymen, Mr. Gardiner and his family in a few months, left his new home and moved to Cerro Gordo county in Iowa. Nearly four years were spent in this latter place, during which time they enjoyed a reasonable degree of prosperity, and the children of the family grew up towards the season of maturity and usefulness. Not yet, however, having found the object of their wishes, whatever that might have been, another and a last move was made by the family, to another part of the State.

CHAPTER III.

> "And thus an airy point he won,
> Where gleaming with the setting sun,
> One burnished sheet of living gold,
> Loch Katrine lay beneath him rolled;
> In all her length far winding lay,
> With promontory, creek and bay,
> And Islands that empurpled bright,
> Floated amid the lovelier light
> And mountains that like giants stand,
> To sentinel enchanted land."—*Lady of the Lake.*

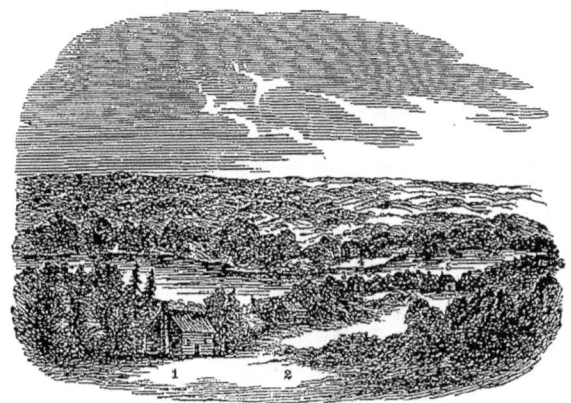

"Spirit Lake," on the North-West boundary of Iowa.
No. 1, Mr. Gardiner's; No. 2, Mr. Luce's; No. 3, Mr. Mattock's; No. 4, Mr. Granger's; No. 5, Mr. Noble's; No. 6, Mr. Thatcher's.

It was in July, 1856, that the hills around Spirit Lake, on the northern boundary of Iowa, first echoed the woodman's axe. Seldom before this, had the numerous beauties of this lovely lake greeted the eye of a white man. Its waters had slept for centuries, unknown to the turmoils of civilization, and disturbed only by its finny inhabitants, flocks of water-fowl, or the rippling of the Indian canoe. Schools of perch, bass, pike, pickerel, trout, and all the luscious fish common to this region, had long gamboled without fear of the white man below its transparent surface, while the swan, proudly curved her graceful neck and floated her snowy bosom above them, exulting in a spot where she reigned sole monarch. The kingfisher, however, often frightened the smaller fish, when, with lightning speed, he swooped from his airy flight, and stole away one of their number, at the same time dimpling the smooth face of the lake and sending the rippling circles wide, to tell the tale of his theft. The thickets on the shores, kindly concealed the nests of many excellent game, and sent forth flocks of wild geese and ducks, while in the tops of the trees, there often lodged and bred the wild pigeon that abounds in the North West.

Two points of land seemed to stretch towards one another, from opposite banks of the lake and only prevented from collision by the waters which lovingly embraced them. Many a graceful bay seemed playfully to chase the retiring banks, while to atone for its intrusion, it smilingly reflected every tree, rock, shrub, and flower, that bent over its surface, and doubled every cloud and flying thing that divided the air above it.

At night, when the visitors of day were not there to see, and the shadowy reflections in the lake clothed it with the soft witchery of spirit-land, the chaste moon, attended by the train of modest stars, was wont to come and bathe in the refreshing waters and then trip hastily away before the light of day. And in the morning and evening, it seemed to be the special pride of the lake to glow with the imparted brilliancy of the sun, when he threw her a golden mantle to wear while he enjoyed his rising and setting dip.

Such was the charming sheet of water near which Mr. Rowland Gardiner chose his last settlement. Truly its loveliness was enough to reward him for his previous toil and changes, and he felt that here, at last, he might settle down, *and spend the evening of his days in a quiet home.*

> "In all my wanderings round this world of care,
> In all my griefs,—and God has given my share—
> I still had hopes my latest hours to crown,
> Amidst these humble bowers to lay me down ;
> To husband out life's taper at the close,
> And keep the flame from wasting by repose ;
> I still had hopes, for pride attends us still,
> Amidst the swains to show my book-learned skill,
> Around my fire an evening group to draw,
> And tell of all I felt and all I saw ;
> And as a hare, whom hounds and horns pursue,
> Pants to the place from whence at first she flew,
> I still had hopes, my long vexations past,
> Here to return and die at home at last."

SETTLERS AT THE LAKE.

Mr. Gardiner was the first to settle on this site, and with his family, was the only settler for some time, within twenty miles of the lake. His eldest daughter, Mary, having married a Mr. Luce, in New York, moved with her father, to this spot, her husband and two small children accompanying them. One snug little log cabin, hewed and dovetailed into shape by the strong arms of Messrs. Gardiner and Luce, and standing on the south side of the lake, was their first abode here, and was well filled. Mr. and Mrs. Gardiner, with their three unmarried children, Eliza, Abigail and Rowland, besides Mr. and Mrs. Luce with their two little ones, comprized the inmates of its sturdy walls. As soon as time would permit, Mr. Luce commenced to erect another log cabin near by, for himself and his little family, that he might no longer crowd the home of his father-in-law, and yet might be always at hand for mutual assistance and protection. As July was too late a month for the planting of Spring crops, little could be done before the approach of winter, beyond the breaking up of some prairie land for Fall crops, and providing shelter and necessaries for themselves and cattle. Thus, not yet able to supply themselves from their new lands, they were dependent on Fort Dodge, eighty miles south-east of Spirit Lake, for all their provisions.

Not long, however, were these two families thus alone in their beautiful location. The news of its rich prairie lands and inviting scenery, soon brought several adventurers to join them, so that by the eighth of March, 1857, there were no less than six families within a few miles of Mr. Gardiner's first cabin. The lake being almost divided in the middle by the opposite shores running out to a point from either side, north and south, and joining under water so as to make a shallow ford, Mr. Granger's family settled north of this ford, immediately opposite Mr. Mattock's cabin, which stood south of the water. Mr. Thatcher built at the east end of the lake, four miles from Mr. Gardiner's. Mr. Luce built about one-quarter of a mile east of his father-in-law, but never finished his dwelling, and Mr. Marble and Mr. Noble provided for themselves also near the lake. The western section of the lake was four miles long and varied in width. The eastern section being somewhat smaller. Thirty-four persons, men, women and children, be besides several men who kept bachelor's hall in a cabin by themselves, thus composed the settlement of Spirit Lake, before the chief scene of this history transpired.

In the peaceful and engaging occupation necessary in their new homes, in felling the trees, building their cabins, and furnishing them with all the comforts they would hold, in breaking up the new land, providing for their cattle, laying in their stocks of fuel against the cold, in the pleasing sports of hunting and fishing, (which latter useful sport, Miss Abigail Gardiner often enjoyed,) the abundant game generously supplied by the waters and banks of the lake, in teaching their children to read and write, and in talking over the toils of the past and the rich prospects of the future, these settlers past the Autmn of 1856, and the first two months of 1857, without anything to disturb the natural course of their lives.

While the abundant game of the region rejoiced them that they were in a wild country, the Indians who visited them were at first not quite so agreeable. But these seeming to regard the new settlers with friendship, and to welcome them to the shores of their enchanting lake, our little band of six families soon laid aside all fear, and associated with them freely. Thus, apparently, at peace with the only being at all to be feared, well and abundantly fed by the wild game they so enjoyed to hunt, carrying out all their darling plans, and full of the brightest hope, this happy people lived some months under the sunshine of a smiling prosperity that shed its blessings on their little settlement.

> "Motion was in their days, rest in their slumbers,
>   And cheerfulness the handmaid of their toil;
> Nor yet too many nor too few their numbers;
>   Corruption could not make their heart his soil;
> The lust which stings, the splendor which encumbers;
>   With the free foresters divide no spoil;
> Serene, not sullen, were the solitudes
>   Of this unsighing people of the woods."

Little did they dream of the awful cloud about to burst over their innocent heads; little imagine that their peaceful and happy homes should soon swim with their own blood and that of their beloved wives and tender children, and become the scene of the foulest, most savage barbarity, ever recorded on the bloody page of history.

CHAPTER IV.

> "In the lodge that glimmers yonder,
> In the little star that twinkles
> Through the vapors on the left hand,
> Lives the envious Evil Spirit."—*Hiawatha*.

WHILE a great part of our nation is agitated with sympathy for the suffering sons of Africa, a growing interest is evident among us in the social, intellectual and moral state of the Indians. Many among the red denizens of our western prairies, after having been driven to their present territories, and suffered everything from the hands of the whites that a strong and proud race ever inflicted on weak neighbors, are naturally exasperated, and like old king Philip, of New England, and Opechanchanough of Virginia, long to become the perpetrators, instead of the victims of extermination. The half-civilized and degraded half breeds, who move continually in advance of the surveyed government lands, and disgrace the name of white man, in their bestial kind of life, are the go-betweens which clear the track for the car of human progress. The horrid mission they perform, is to fire every beastly passion to which the Indians are prone, so that they may consume themselves as quickly as possible by their own vices. Well would it be for this low race of whites, could they thus subdue the savage by vice, without being themselves its most luckless victims.

Intoxicating drink is the chief article we export to the Indian, in order that he may the more easily be removed from our way. So addicted, indeed, are the wretched savages to drunkenness and its attendant vices, that multitudes of them die from its effects, before the natural age, and that they are encouraged in this suicidal tendency by the general policy of the whites towards them, is a fact of notoriety wherever their history is known.

A movement is now in progress in New York, in favor of ameliorating the lamentable condition of the Indians, but as it seems to be purely benevolent, and not the work of interested politicans, its success is rather doubtful. Certainly if there are on the globe any who have a claim upon our benevolence, they are the Aborogines of our land, for to them we owe the best territory from which they, its possessors by right of nature, are swiftly passing away.

Can it be, that our nation will never atone for the wrong she has done the poor Indian? Or is the hand of retributive justice already felt in the many political strifes and anarchical tendencies that convulse and sometimes almost rend the country in twain? Though the eastern borders of Iowa and Minnesota are no longer the fixed homes of savages, their territories further West, are as yet continually infested by them. The Indians roam freely over those vast prairies, and ften approach and even mingle with the white settlers. Thus, they have in many things, become civilized, and not a few of them have embraced Christianity. Rev. J. L. Breck, in Minnesota Territory, has been wonderfully successful in his mission to the Indians, but yet there are many tribes entirely ignorant of the arts of civilization or the morality of religion. The Indians in this part of the country go chiefly by the name of Yanktons and Sioux, and are professedly at peace with our government, from whom they derive small but regular payments through the Indian agents.

The Sioux is a widely spread tribe, found in all parts of the West beyond the western borders of Missouri, and with the exception of a small band known as "*Ink-pa-du-ta's Band*," are friendly to the whites. This small band, led by Ink-pa-du-ta, is outlawed by the tribe of Sioux, and is noted for its roving and continual depredations on the whites. They live only by game and plunder, and luxuriate in the most shocking barbarities. In their depredations, they are thought to be secretly encouraged by the friendly Sioux and Yankton's, though the latter profess to the whites to condemn them.

On the *Jaques* or James river, a branch of the Missouri, named in its upper portion, Tchansansan, which sweeps its noble flood through the prairies north-west and west of Spirit Lake, is an encampment of the Yankton's containing one hundred and ninety lodges. Here the Ink-pa-du-ta band at times retire when laden with booty, and find such encouragement or opposition as the wily Yanktons think it their policy to exhibit.

From somewhere in this direction the Ink-pa-du-tas made an expedition towards Iowa, in the early part of this year. Through forest and fen, over rivers and lakes, through prairies and wild lonely trails, they wound their tortuous path and reached the neighborhood of Spirit Lake, in the first week of March. By the evening of the seventh of March, under the cover of the winter's night, the savage band had cleared the snow from sufficient ground on which to pitch their nine lodges. Here we leave them for the present. The

HUNGRY VISITORS. 15

warriors, fourteen in number, holding bloody council in the tent of their leader, Ink-pa-du-ta, while the squaws and papooses are resting themselves in their other lodges.

Through the long hours of that night, when the unsuspecting settlers were wrapped in peaceful repose, the cold winds that soughed sadly through the tops of the naked trees and whistled mercilessly around the rough corners of their substantial warm cabins, told them not of the foul conspiracy that was brewing

> "In the lodge that glimmered yonder,"
> Among "the envious evil" spirits.
> While "these stood there in their council,
> With their weapons and their war-gear,
> Painted like the leaves of Autumn,
> Painted like the sky of morning,
> Wildly glaring at each other;
> In their faces stern defiance;
> In their hearts the feuds of ages,
> The hereditary hatred,
> The ancestral thirst of vengeance."

CHAPTER V.

"O barbarous and bloody spectacle!"—*Shakspeare.*

COLDLY on the settlers of Spirit Lake dawned the morning of Sunday, March 8th, 1857! Thickly lay the snow round their cabins, and on the still surface of the lake, now bound in the chains of its ice-death. As the frost had already begun to melt on the panes of Mr. Gardiner's windows with the heat of the morning fire, the family were just about to surround the welcome breakfast that lay steaming invitingly on the table, when a solitary Indian unexpectedly walked into the house, and begged for a morsel of bread!

No sooner had the hunger of this first visitor been satisfied, than another came on like errand, and was followed by others of his band so soon, that in a few minutes all fourteen of Ink-pa-du-ta's warriors whom we left last night in savage council, had crowded the little cabin and swallowed the breakfast that had been prepared for the frightened family!

The Indians were generously supplied with food by the astonished proprietors of the cabin, who could now see at some distance the nine lodges, with two men and children standing about them.

There not being enough provision to supply all the savages, they behaved less friendly than usual, and gradually growing fierce, siezed Mr. Gardiner's gun, extracted the ball, and demanded his percussion caps which he readily gave them. These they emptied into their pockets and tossed back the box insultingly. Ink-pa-du-ta's son required Mr. Luce to hand out more bread, but on learning that their supplies were nearly exhausted, he pointed his gun towards Mr. Luce and was about to fire, when the latter prevented him by a sudden strong grasp of the weapon. At this, all the Indians left the house with every sign of indignation, which they at first vented on the cattle. Mr. Gardiner owned with his son-in-law, only six head of cattle, which the Indians drove away without resistance on the part of the family, and wantonly *shot!*

For the last few days the settlers had been preparing to send to Fort Dodge, for provisions, as they were nearly out, but the Indians seemed convinced that more booty could be found, and were resolved to have it at any cost.

Seeing that the barbarians were meditating an attack, Mr. Gardiner said that the families must all meet in one house for greater safety. The house selected for that purpose was Mr. Mattock's, one mile east of Mr. Gardiner's, as it was larger, stronger and better suited for defence. But no time was allowed them, for before the women had put on their bonnets and decided which route would best conceal them from the foe, the cry of "*they come! they come!*" paralyzed all their movements, as eleven of the warriors again entered and demanded all the flour in the house. While Mr. Gardiner was in the act of getting it for them he was fatally shot, and fell down dead instantly! His breathless wife was shot immediately afterward and cruelly scalped.

As there was but one large room in the house, and the whole party of Indians densely crowded it, the shocking deaths of the parents were not seen by the innocent and frightened children who were huddled together in speechless horror in the corner. Thus their tender hearts were mercifully spared the sight of their dying parents, who, however, were soon followed to the world of spirits by nearly all who were dear to them on earth. Mr. Luce had gone out to the house of a neighbor, so that he did not witness this awful beginning of the bloody massacre, and was even deprived the consolation of fighting for his wife and two young children before yielding up his own life. His poor wife was the next victim to the vengeance of the savages, for she was shot while convulsively but in silent agony clasping her tender babe to her bosom.

The infant, however, was not long left an orphan. The fatal war club dashed out its little brains, as also those of its brother and young uncle, Rowland Gardiner. Struck dumb with inexpressible fright, overwhelmed and paralized with the suddenness and horror of the bloody attack, all these unfortunate victims perished in breathless silence and without one effort of resistance. All this time, Miss Abigail Gardiner, a girl of only fifteen, stood motionless and silent, transfixed in helpless terror, and unaccountably was spared from death. Her sister, Miss Eliza, fortunately, was not at home, having gone a few days before to the neighborhood of Fort Dodge, with the family of a Mr. Strong. Thus the timid and shrinking Abigail was the only one of the family in the cabin alive, while her dear Father and Mother and little brother Rowland, her married sister, Mrs. Luce, with the two babes, were left weltering in their own and each others blood. Being savagely commanded to follow her devilish captors to their camp, she slowly and timidly obeyed, too much oppressed with sorrow for her relatives to be very anxious about her own fate.

Meanwhile, Mr. Luce, and a neighbor, Mr. Clarke, were shot down, while near the house of Mr. Mattock; they were preparing for an expedition to Fort Dodge. After dragging to their camp together with the afflicted Abagail, all they could carry from the house, some of the barbarians rested for about one day in their lodges, while a party of eight, again sallied forth to attack the other families of the little settlement. Twelve more souls—men, women and children—fell victims to their fury, and two women, Mrs. Thatcher and Mrs. Noble, were brought captives to the camp. These last two joined the lonely Abigail on the ninth. What an interval of pain, anxiety, grief and apprehension must that have been for so young and inexperenced a lady, between the commencement of her captivity on the eighth, and the time of her being joined on the ninth by Mrs. Thatcher and Mrs. Noble! Sick at heart from the scenes of bloodshed she had witnessed, with only one relative living and she far away, over excited and not able to sleep from nervousness, and without a bed suitable for a civilized being if she could have slept, surrounded by the fiendish murderers of all those she loved best on earth, not knowing what her own fate might be, whether the scalping-knife, starvation, desertion to the merciless winter, or the more welcome gun-shot should terminate her now wretched life, with all the warm and pleasing prospects of youth thus nipped off in the bud and nothing to look forward to but vague horrors perhaps greater than those of the past, her situation was one of indescribable affliction. No kind father could ever more bid her an affectionate good-night; no dear mother could ever again smooth her moistened pillow, or kiss away her tears; never again should her dear little brother and she enjoy the fishing in that lovely lake, or gambol 'neath the tall trees, chasing the rabbits into their holes at the roots, and the squirrels up to their hiding places in the branches, or assist their parents in their work; never again should that once happy family assemble round to share the common meal; never again in the long winter evenings sit round the blazing fire, listening to reading, or talking and laughing over the cares and plays of the day; and last and most grievous of all, never again on earth could their loved voices mingle in the evening hymn of praise, and their dear father read and expound the daily chapter and commend them solemnly in prayer to the Divine protection.

> "For them no more the blazing hearth shall burn,
> Or busy housewife ply her evening care;
> No children run to lisp their sires return,
> Or climb his knees the envied kiss to share."

Oh! how full, to bursting, must the tender young heart of Abigail have been that awful night! What marvel were it if she buried her streaming eyes in her hands while she lay sleepless on her comfortless lair and prayed to God! leave me not thus *alone!* O God! *wilt* Thou leave me thus *alone?* ALONE!!

CHAPTER VI.

> Better end here unborn. Why is life given
> To be thus wrested from us? rather why
> Obtruded on us thus? who if we knew
> What we receive, would either not accept
> Life offered, or soon beg to lay it down,
> Glad to be dismissed in peace.— *Milton.*

ON the fifth day after the capture of Abigail, and the fourth after that of Mrs. Thatcher and Mrs. Noble, another unfortunate victim was added to their gloomy society. Mrs. Marble, who lived a few miles off, had been spared from murder herself at that time, after seeing her dear husband ruthlessly slaughtered, her children dashed in pieces, and her loved home, stained with their precious blood, and thoroughly sacked. Thus by the evening of the thirteenth, the camp of the savages was glutted with the spoils of the ruined settlement, and was graced by the downcast looks of four fair white captives. These had been spared from butchery indeed, but not in mercy. A living death was in reserve for them; a *living death* whose horrors are far beyond the powers of this feeble pen fitly to describe.

Would that it might feel the power of a Shakspeare, would that it might be kindled with the fire of a Byron, that it might do justice to the unutterable woes suffered by these four fair survivors of this awful massacre.

After having spilled out on the weird shores of Spirit Lake, more than forty human souls in all, and left their slaughtered and mangled bodies gory in their blood, exposed to the ravages of weather and wild beasts, the barbarians started on their homeward journey on the morning of the fourteenth of March, 1857.

The Indians had come to Spirit Lake with two horses, each harnessed to a sleigh. In one of these sleighs they placed Miss Gardiner as driver during the first two days of their journey, loading it heavily with plunder and papooses. The other captives were at the outset compelled to walk, though the weather was cruelly cold, and the snow deep. But after the first two days, Miss Gardiner was ordered to give up her seat in the sleigh to others, and to walk. Meanwhile a party of twelve warriors left the company and set off towards the river Desmoines, for the avowed purpose of perpetrating another massacre on a settlement of whites. These twelve were absent on their mission of death two days, and returned laden with spoil of every variety. Dry goods, groceries, with tea, sugar, coffee, flour, vegetables, powder, lead, muskets, pistols, and twelve horses, were the principal articles of their plunder. They reported on their return that they had killed only one woman to secure all this property, but from other and more reliable accounts we learn that as many as *twelve* unfortunate whites had in that expedition fallen victims to their cruelty. It was not enough that the poor captives had been deprived of all their relatives and civilized society. Their captives compelled them to relinquish even their own clothing and assume the costume of barbarians.

They oiled and braided the hair of the white women on both sides, and painted their faces! This however, was not till about three weeks had been passed in their wearisome comfortless journey. Having paused in their march in order to make this important change in the appearance of their victims and increase their discomfort, they resumed it by making still heavier the griefs of their already broken hearts:

> "O the long and dreary winter!
> O the cold and cruel winter!
> Ever thicker, thicker, thicker,
> Froze the ice on lake and river,
> Ever deeper, deeper, deeper,
> Fell the snow on all the landscape,
> Fell the covering snow, and drifted
> Through the forest round the pathway!"

CHAPTER VII.

> " O the wasting of the famine !
> O the wailing of the children !
> O the anguish of the women !
> All the earth was sick and famished ;
> Hungry was the air around them,
> Hungry was the sky above them,
> And the hungry stars in heaven,
> Like the eyes of wolves, glared at them."—*Hiawatha.*

AFTER the adoption of the Indian costumes by the captives, their hardships were every way increased. They were compelled to carry *as they trudged through the snow, heavy burdens on their backs.* And the weight of these was augmented from day to day, as the poor women were able to bear them, and even when they were not sufficiently strong. The contents of Miss Gardiner's "*pack*" were eight bars of lead, one pint of leaden balls for shooting buffalo, one tent cover, made of the thickest, heaviest kind of cloth, one common bed comforter, one Indian blanket, one iron bar about four feet long and an inch thick, a stick of wood, the use of which she was unable to determine, and yet of considerable weight, a very heavy gun, and in addition to all this, a flat piece of wood about four feet long, to keep the back straight. When the reader considers these articles attentively, and remembers that a tender maiden of only fifteen summers was compelled to carry them for days and weeks in the snow, and that, often when she was half sick from cold and want of proper nourishment, and when he remembers too, how little we allow even many of our women to perform in civilized countries, how they need horses and carriages to take them even small distances, and must be humored in every way, as the weaker vessel, he may realize in some faint degree, what this poor young girl was compelled to suffer.

The load laid upon the other captives may be guessed at from this of Miss Gardiner. If the youngest among them had such an enormous weight, nearly *seventy* pounds, what must have been imposed on the older, married ladies ? Besides the weight enumerated, and the inexpressible anguish of having lost all her dear relatives but one, in that horrid massacre, Miss Gardiner had to bear up against continual threats of death. For every night she was compelled to comply with the orders of her tyrant, by the threat that she should be killed the next morning!

But their oft repeated threats, in time, lost their terrors, and she was able to sink into her needful repose, in utter indifference to her fate. The Indian men would not assist Miss Gardiner in putting the pack on her back, and at times, when her strength had failed, she had to carry it to a fallen tree in order to raise it on her back. At times, the squaws assisted her.

The spoils from the settlement lasted the savages and their prey, for about four weeks. After this they were supplied by chance by the duck and geese, which appeared as Spring advanced. These, however, soon failed them, and left the improvident travelers nothing but wild artichokes, such as they might find in their journey.

During the period of this hap-hazard kind of living, the ladies endured much keener suffering, the pangs of hunger being added to all the rest.

"O the wasting of the famine!
O the wailing of the children!
O the anguish of the women!"

As an illustration of their mode of living at this time, Miss Gardiner relates an interesting anecdote. She says that she and several squaws were sent out to hunt game, and could find nothing but the empty hole of a skunk in the bank of a lake, and she was told by her fellow hunters to go in quest of a switch with which to kill the animal *for food* (!) when it should return to its home.

Now, hungry as the poor young lady was, she thought she was not yet so far gone as to have any relish for a pole-cat, and so she set her woman wits to work, to find a way of escape. She concluded to be so long in search of the required switch, as to give the savory prey abundant time to re-enter his hole before her return, and thus escape his pursuers, and she was rejoiced in the success of her stratagem. She found on bringing the switch, that the squaws had allowed him to enter and escape their grasp uninjured, and despaired of ever killing him and enjoying his delicious flesh! But after some days thus living from precarious supplies, the party was relieved by herds of buffalo, which scoured the prairie far and wide. Yet though the Indians fed themselves abundantly, the unfortunate prisoners fared no better than before.

Many times Miss Gardiner was compelled to go without a morsel of food for forty-eight hours, and yet carried her burden as usual. The captive ladies had, for the first three weeks, been kept together in one tent, but afterward, lest they might afford consolation to each other, they were partitioned out among the different lodges, and separated one from the other, and exchanged around. Thus Miss Gardiner was enslaved by six different families, or served in six different tents by turns, during the three months of her captivity.

After six weeks of regular, uninterrupted marching through forests and swamps, across rivers, lakes, and prairies, the band reached the Big Sioux River.

Murder of Mrs. Thatcher by Ink-pa-du-ta's band, by pushing her from a log into the river and then shooting her.

CHAPTER VIII.

> "To die—to sleep—
> No more; and, by a sleep, to say we end
> The heart ache, and the thousand natural shocks
> That flesh is heir to; 'tis a consummation
> Devoutly to be wished.—*Shakspeare.*

THINK not, kind reader, that you have yet passed the direst horrors of this dreadful tragedy. There await for your perusal, barbarities as black, and cruelties as foul as those we have recorded, or indeed have ever been written by mortal man. Nor pause here, palled and sickened by the painful details. If thou shalt be led to thankfulness for thy own condition, and to pity the misfortunes of others, thou shalt not have read this sad history in vain.

Deep, broad and swift are the waters of the Big Sioux River, where our party had to cross. The trees on the banks bow luxuriantly over the current, and seem trying at times, to kiss their own shadows in the depths beneath them. In the winds that sweep up and down the stream, they proudly toss their heavy boughs, and boldly lave them in the flood when the river overflows its banks, but they often fall headlong into the torrent, rooted up by the working of the waters, and pulled down by the force of the winds. Thus, matted rafts of fallen timber are found in the river which sometimes form very convenient bridges. On one of these bridges our party had to cross, and here transpired one of the most brutal acts of the whole history.

Mrs. Thatcher, one of the captives, was a woman of very delicate health, and on that account had not been charged by the Indians with any burden. But even the marching, at that inclement season, and in the snows, was more than any woman could be expected to endure, and much less so frail a person as was Mrs. Thatcher. The marching so exhausted her strength that all her limbs became very much swoolen, and the veins in them *burst out on the surface!!* Her sufferings were intense, but still she endeavored to persevere on her painful march. With a desperate effort to sustain herself, she followed with bleeding limbs and faltering step, those who led the way across the bridge of cold, wet, slippery logs and flood-wood. Every nerve was in the highest state of excitement, every muscle of her face quivered with pain, her soul was nigh unto bursting with anguish, and needing everything that can be done to aid and relieve a sufferer, and yet there she was, compelled to risk her life without a single helping hand, on that dangerous, uncertain bridge, on which, if a single slip should be made, she would be precipitated instantly into the yawning black flood below!

Just as she was over the deepest part of the river, a fiendish Indian suddenly pushed her from the logs into the water! the *cold*, icy water! This was done with an air of impatience and disgust, as if the pityless ruffian was glad of the chance to get rid of one who could neither bear his burdens nor glut his passions.

With incredible effort, such as one so weak can only make when nerved by the fear of death, the unfortunate woman reached the shore, and was clinging to the roots at the bank, benumbed with cold, and almost fainting from her exertion, when her diabolical tormentors *beat her off from the shore with their clubs without mercy!!* Nor did their brutality to her end here, for after the flood had carried her beyond the reach of their clubs, they shot her, and thus put an end to her tortures.

CHAPTER IX.

Soon may this fluttering spark of vital flame
Forsake its languid melancholy frame!
Soon may these eyes their trembling lustre close,
Welcome the dreamless night of long repose!
Soon may this wo-worn spirit seek the bourn
Where lulled to slumber, grief forgets to mourn!—Camp.

GLADLY would this pen drop here from the writer's hand, tired and sick of tracking the bloody trail of these savage murderers, but justice to the sufferers, justice to the survivors, and justice to the public, whose sympathies for the victims of Spirit Lake Massacre have been stirred to the depths, all require the finishing of this painful task. Would that the last death scene had been described! would that I had already narrated the last foul crime whose record stains these pages!

Pursuing their journey still westward, the barbarian horde with their three remaining victims (Miss A. Gardiner, Mrs. Noble and Mrs. Marble,) reached a small sheet of water called Skunk Lake. Here they paused for a short time and pitched their camp and were visited by two Indians of the Lac-qui-parle tribe who entered their camp with some important proposals. They treated earnestly during two days with the Ink-pa-du-ta band, offering to purchase Mrs. Marble, that they might return her to the whites and claim the ransom which had been offered for her. After protracted deliberations, they bought her, giving in return several horses, quantities of powder, lead, &c.

Thus deprived by death and barter of these two fellow captives, Miss Gardiner and Mrs. Noble, were left to drag out the remnant of their wretched captivity without them. Mrs. Marble had a safe journey and obtained an early ransom Not so, as yet, the other two, left with the Ink-pa-du-tas! They now pursued a more northerly course, with their cruel conductors, who lessened their tyranny in nothing.

Besides the regular task of carrying her burden, Miss Gardiner (who bore up under her trials with unusual fortitude and strength,) was compelled to haul water, cut wood, help pitch tents at night, to make the bread and to bake it. And yet, whenever any one was stinted from scarcity, that one was sure to be Miss Gardiner! The

Israelites, compelled to make bricks without straw, were hardly more unjustly treated than was she, for she was obliged to make bread without what civilized women generally think indispensable. On being asked what she made the bread with, she replied, "I raised it with water, and baked it in a fryingpan over a fire in the tent." "Make the doors upon a woman's wit and it will out at the casement; shut that, and 'twill out at the key-hole; stop that, 'twill fly out at the chimney." Miss Gardiner seemed gifted with peculiar strength to perform her arduous labors and great tact in accommodating herself to those who deserved at her hands anything but submission and kind service. Like every woman who understands the secret of her sex's power, (in the words of Lamb,) she

> "Most hid the strength that most subdued;
> To gain each end, its opposite pursued,
> Lured by neglect, advanced by delay,
> And gained command by swearing to obey."

Far differently constituted was her more unfortunate friend, Mrs. Noble. She was a woman of unyielding temper and high spirit. Burning with the wrongs she suffered; conscious of her own superiority to the brutes who tyrannized over her; smarting under the irritating taunts and jeers and frequent *blows* which alone rewarded all her show of independence; desperate respecting her own fate and longing at times to reach "the bourn

> Where lulled to slumber, grief forgets to mourn,"

she made no effort to please her awful masters, but in every way possible, opposed them and refused submission. So outraged were all her finer instincts by their brutalities that she declared with inflexible resolution, that she would "*die*" before she would submit to their commands. Four weeks had now passed in this constant struggle and maddening oppression, since the sale of Mrs. Marble to the Lac-qui-parle Indians, when matters with poor Mrs. Noble reached their climax.

She was lodged in the same tent with the bloody son of Ink-pa-du-ta and Miss Gardiner, when he ordered her to go out of his tent, and thus to spend the night exposed to the chilly airs and damp ground of spring. Exasperated beyond all control and reckless of her fate, the enraged woman declared she would *die* before she would obey his cruel order. The savage threatened to kill her if disobedient, but she repeated her resolve to "perish rather than submit," upon which he took her by the hand and led her out of the tent. Then piteous groans and sounds of merciless blows reached the ears of Miss Gardiner, who was left alone almost *crazed* with wrath and fear, within the loathed tent, while the awful work of death was proceeding without.

While Mrs. Noble was writhing under the insufferable agony of the repeating blows of the murderous barbarian, what wonder if

> "Then flashed the living lightning from her eyes,
> And screams of horror rend the affrighted skies;
> Not louder shrieks to pitying Heaven are cast,
> When husbands or dear infants breathe their last."

The devilish deed accomplished, the murderer re-entered the tent, washed his gory hands in the presence of Miss Gardiner (who sat pale and motionless with terror,) boasted that he had dispatched Mrs. Noble, and then retired to rest.

> "Nothing can we call our own but DEATH!"

CHAPTER X.

> Auspicious Hope! In thy sweet garden grow
> Wreaths for each toil, a charm for every woe;
> Won by their sweets, in Nature's languid hour,
> The way-worn pilgrim seeks thy summer bower;
> There as the wild bee murmurs on the wing,
> What peaceful dreams thy handmaid spirits bring!
> What viewless forms the Æolian organ play,
> And sweep the furrowed lines of anxious thought away!

READER, we have now passed the last scene of murder in this sad history. One death more will be recorded before we close; but that is not one of an innocent victim, but suffered justly by a savage, and therefore will excite us only with feelings of satisfaction.

Deprived by Mrs. Noble's death, of the last soul left to sympathize even by look or gesture in her trials, how deep and manifoldly increased must have been the sorrow endured by the lonely Abigail!— For

> "The heart hath treble wrong,
> When it is barr'd the aidance of expression."

ANOTHER SHOCK.

Indeed, the more we know of her sufferings and feel how pitilessly they were increased, we only wonder that the young girl lost neither her health nor her reason.

She arose the next morning from her lair with an awful weight upon her spirit, as when one wakes unrefreshed to a scene of present and future WOE! But she was obliged to go on, with the prospect of dragging out indefinitely a precarious existence more painful than death. Would she be the next victim to their fiendish thirst for blood? Could she expect to hold up much longer under those dreadful hardships? And when she began to fail, would her former service and obedience bespeak the compassion of those inhuman murderers? No! She had no mercy to expect from them—only unmitigated oppression to end with nothing short of a bloody death.

In going out of the tent that sad morning, after the heart-rending scenes of the last chapter, all nature seemed to her to be heavy with guilt or scorn. The sun rose in blood and shed a lurid light through the trees as if loth to remove the veil of night from the mangled body of the murdered dead—as if grudging to such fiends of darkness as Ink-pa-du-ta's band, the welcome salute of his morning ray. The air was damp and clammy; not a breath of wind relieved the crushing stillness of the forest; not a breeze sighed through the branches. Grief and unutterable indignation had frozen every feature of Nature's face into an inflexible frown,—

> "And lo! the universal air
> Seemed lit with ghastly flame;—
> Ten thousand thousand dreadful eyes
> Were looking down in blame:"

And near the tent lay the gory corpse of her last fellow prisoner, so horrid and disfigured by her abuses that the sight was intolerable to the heart-broken Abigail. She turned impulsively away from the dreadful sight and prepared reluctantly for the day's march. After they had fairly started, one more shock was in store for Miss Gardiner. One of the warriors as if not yet sated with blood, turned back and discharged into the face of the corpse the contents of a Colt's revolver! This gratuitous show of barbarism over, the travelers pursued their way. About this time it was that Miss Gardiner began to lose count of the days. At first the captives remembered Sundays and strove to keep them in spite of difficulties; but when deprived of every Christian companion, and passing day after day, repeating the same round of monotonous weary toil, and sullen silence, Miss Gardiner lost her reckoning of the names of the days. She had some books, however, and occasionally could snatch a moment to read; but the comfort from this source was very slight, owing to the unremitting fatigue of her body which hindered the action of her mind.

She was allowed no covering for her head but grease. Even in the coldest weather, the Indians allowed nothing warmer to her. But they filled her hair with oil from any animal they had killed, and after braiding it, left it thus for days; and as the spring advanced, the burning of this oil into her defenceless head, by the sun heat, was added to all the other trials of our unfortunate heroine.

Her own shoes had been taken away from her, as from all the captives after the first three weeks of their journey, and moccasins were supplied them. These proved warm and comfortable for walking in winter, and (no doubt contrary to the wishes of the Indians,) were better for them than shoes.

Nothing further of special interest happened in the journey till the party reached the Yankton encampment on the Jaques River, which has been mentioned in a former chapter. The distance of this point, to Skunk Lake, (according to a western paper,) was estimated to be about one hundred and fifty miles. The route had run in a northwestern direction, generally, but was winding and crooked. All the journey but the latter part, had been performed on the snows, and in bitter cold, but Spring softened the rigors of the journey towards the end.

On arriving at the camp, the captive was sold by Ink-pa-du-ta to the Yanktons, who profess to be friendly to the whites, but did not in the least ameliorate the condition, or lighten the burdens of Miss Gardiner. An idea of the severity, cruelty, and wickedness of the Indians may be inferred from the fact, that of the fourteen horses possessed by Ink-pa-du-ta's band in the early part of their march, only *one*, (that stolen from Dr. Harriott, at the lake,) survived and reached the Yankton camp. Here she continued to endure the same slavery, until her final ransom by the whites. Meantime, any change must have encouraged her to hope for freedom, and this hope we shall find was fully realized.

> O liberty, thou goddess, heavenly bright,
> Profuse of bliss and pregnant with delight!
> Eternal pleasures in thy presence reign,
> And smiling plenty leads thy wanton train.

CHAPTER XI.

"Here the lamented dead in dust shall lie,
Life's lingering languors o'er, its labors done;
Where waving boughs, between the earth and sky,
Admit the farewell radiance of the sun."—*W. G. Clark.*

MEANTIME, rumor had carried to the inhabitants of Fort Dodge and many other places, the direful news of Spirit Lake massacre, and excited the wrath and sympathies of all who heard it. Flaming editorials in many newspapers, spread the feeling far and wide in the country, and loud and moving was the demand for relief to the captives, and vengeance on the murderers. A party of about ten troops set out from Fort Dodge on the 27th or 28th of March, for Spirit Lake. But so insufferable was the cold, that they returned after having buried one man only.

Another party of twenty-three men started at a later date, and were assisted in their humane mission by Capt. I. C. Johnson, of Company C, of Webster City, and William Burckholder, Esq., of Company A, who came with others, from Granger Claims, twelve miles east of Spirit Lake. Theirs was the melancholy duty of interring the dead, who had for some weeks lain where they had fallen under the bloody scalping-knives, battle-axes, or still more murderous rifles of the Indians.

The persons whom they buried were Mr. A. Noble, Mr. J. M. Thatcher, with his child; E. Riam, Mrs. Joel Howe and her five children, a man found at Granger's, and supposed to be one of that name, and W. W. Mattocks, with his wife and five children; Robert Clark, of Waterloo, in the State of Iowa; Dr. I. H. Harriott, (son of Dr. Harriott, of Indiana;) J. H. Cropper, supposed by some to be one of the Grangers; a man, name unknown; Rowland Gardiner, wife and child, six years old; Mrs. Mary Luce, (daughter of Mr. Gardiner,) with her husband and two children, Albert and Amanda.

All these bodies were found lying where they had fallen, except that of Dr. Harriott, which was found leaning up against a tree with a rifle in his hands. Miss Gardiner says it was so placed by the Indians for a ruse, that it might seem as if resistance had been made by the whites. So little resistance, however, had in fact been made, that no Indian was injured except one, who received a slight wound on his leg.

"There calmly let them rest! from friends and kindred. Mid natures solitudes, by stranger hands were the mother and child committed to their last resting place, and many a heart in anguish bled, and many an eye with tear-drops, wept their fate by death untimely sealed."

The bodies of two men partly consumed by fire were found near the ruins of Mattock's house. All bore marks of having received from two to four death shots, and even after life had fled, the marks of violence upon their bodies, only attested the fiend-like spirit of their murderers. Heads partially split open, often severed in twain and from the body and limbs mutilated, were every where exhibited. Not content with the destruction of human life, they felled everything beneath their fury. Between forty and fifty cattle were found killed around the deserted houses, and even for the most part, cut in pieces. The savages fully carried out their determination of utter destruction.

Having performed the last sad rites of burial, and committed to the ground all the human bodies to be found, the party started to return to their homes. Captain Johnson, and Mr. Burckholder, however, disagreeing with their companions respecting the route, parted company, since which, nothing has been heard of them!* Their boots had been frozen so hard at night, that they could not get them on, and they were last observed tearing up their blankets and binding them on their feet. "Burckholder," says the Fort Dodge Sentinel of April 16th, 1857, (from which paper this chapter is extracted almost verbatim,) "has been elected County Recorder in his absence. Both are noble fellows, and we hope and believe they will return."

July 3d. Nothing has been heard from either Johnson or Burckholder. Maj. William Williams, commander of the volunteer expedition which went to Spirit Lake, says in his report of April 13th: "The number killed, including the two burned, was thirty-nine, besides thirteen missing, four of whom are known to be held as captives by the Indians, viz., Mrs. Thatcher, Mrs. Noble, Mrs. Marble and Miss Abigail Gardiner. The probabilities being that the balance of the missing were among the killed."

---

*Appendix, page 48.

CHAPTER XII.

"O'er all confusion marring earth and air,
O'er all the shuddering hours of man's despair,
Still reigns one fixed decree of peace and love,
And still though dim below, 'tis bright above.—*Jno. Sterling.*

WHILE the efforts detailed in the last chapter were being made in Iowa, not less were projected in Minnesota Territory, where the keenest interest was felt in the fate of the captives.

The best mode of their redemption was a very delicate matter to determine, and was long mooted by the leading minds in the Territory. Gov. Medary and Agent C. E. Flandrau, acted with consummate prudence in the premises, as the success of their effort fully proves. As the two Lac-qui-parle Indians who bought Mrs. Noble had brought her into St. Paul, where they received $1,000 for her ransom, four weeks before the release of Miss Gardiner, they reported to the authorities the whereabouts of the latter.

On Saturday, the 23d of May, 1857, three Indians sent out by Agent Flandrau, left the Yellow Medicine Agency on their way to effect the ransom of Miss Gardiner. The names of these friendly men are MA-ZA-IN-TE-MANI, or the man who shoots metal as he walks; HO-TON-WASH-TE, or Beautiful Voice; and CHE-TAN-MAZA, or the Iron Hawk.

The following account is from the *Pioneer Democrat*, June 25th, published in St. Paul, Minnesota Territory:

"On the 27th May, while traveling in the direction of the Big Sioux, they came upon the trail of INK-PA-DU-TA'S band, at a place called by the Indians, 'Big Toad Lake.'

"On the 29th, following up the same trail, they arrived at a recently deserted camp, where they found the dead body of Mrs. NOBLE. The body was terribly mutilated; it was apparent that she had been most cruelly outraged, not only before but after death.

"Three bullet wounds were discovered in her head, and on her limbs and arms, the traces of brutal cruelties were visible. The Indians wrapped her body in a blanket and interred it. MA-ZA-IN-TE-MANI, a Christian Indian, performing those religious services over the grave of the unfortunate victim, dictated by his crude, yet earnest belief in the Christian religion. Leaving this sad place, on the next day the party arrived at another deserted camp, where they found lying upon the ground, Mrs. Noble's hair. It was collected by the Christian Indian referred to, with the intention of bringing it to the Agency, where it could be sent to Mrs. Noble's friends and relatives.

"On the next day, the 30th May, the party arrived at an encampment of one hundred and ninety lodges of the Yankton Sioux, and three lodges of Ink-pa-du-ta's band. On their arrival here they ascertained that Miss Gardiner and Mrs. Noble had been sold by Ink-pa-du-ta's band to a Yankton warrior named WAN-DUS-KA-IHAN-KE, or the End of the Snake, and that a few nights after the sale, a son of Ink-pa-du-ta came to the camp and demanded that the white women should be turned out of the lodge, where they were kept by their purchaser. Upon his refusal to comply, Mrs. Noble was forcibly removed, outraged beyond all power of language to describe, and then brutally murdered."

But to return to the Christian Indian and his associates. Upon arriving at the Yankton camp, they ascertained that Miss Gardiner was at the lodge of the END-OF-THE-SNAKE. They immediately opened negotiations to obtain her release. The END-OF-THE-SNAKE said he had bought her with the intention of restoring her to the whites, but could not give her up until he obtained the consent of the rest of the Yanktons. Councils were then called, at which the propositions of the three WA-PE-TONS was canvassed. One Yankton chief objected to the surrender of Miss Gardiner on the ground that they could do better by conveying her to the Missouri, and selling her to the military officers there; that they could thus get a large amount of powder and tobacco. Councils were held for two or three days, when the Yankton chief was appeased, much in the same manner as many civilized legislators, by a present. No further opposition was made to the purchase of Miss Gardiner, and she was accordingly surrendered to the Christian Indian and his associates, who received at the same time the assurance that the Yankton's held her merely in trust, to be delivered to the whites. The price paid for Miss Gardiner was two horses, seven blankets, two kegs of powder, box of tobacco, and other articles, with which the Indians had been provided by Maj. Flandrau.

As soon as the purchase was completed the (three) Indians went back some distance to a place where they had concealed their wagon and two horses, (knowing that if the Yanktons knew of their having them, they would demand it also with the ransom,) and prepared to start for the Yellow Medicine, two of the End-of-the-Snake's sons volunteering to accompany the WA-PE-TONS to the Agency. But they were somewhat delayed by a feast among the Yankton's to which the captive and her liberators were invited. Miss Gardiner, however, having learned to understand much of the Indian language, (though she could not speak it fluently,) declined to attend, knowing from their conversation, that dog flesh was to be the chief dish on the occasion. And had it not been for the timely assistance of the two Yankton brothers, it is more than likely that the three WA-PE-TONS and Miss Gardiner would never have reached the Agency alive."

The Yankton chief, in addition to many assurances of good will, ordered the two-horse wagon with which the three Christian Indians came, to be loaded with buffalo skins and buffalo meat, so that there was room on the load for only Miss Gardiner. She therefore drove

Miss Gardiner driving the team, conducted by the friendly Indians who had ransomed her.

the horses herself, the five Indians leading the way. Thus, as she had entered on her three months captivity by driving a one-horse sleigh filled with spoil and papooses, for two days, she rode away from the same, driving a triumphant double wagon, *loaded with presents from the Yanktons, drawn by a span of horses!*

"For four days after leaving the Yankton camp, they were followed by a portion of Ink-pa-du-ta's band, but they were evidently deterred from making an attack by the presence of the Yanktons. Twenty days from their departure from the Yellow Medicine Agency, the Indians returned, having been six days making the journey between the Yankton camp and the Agency."

"Some interesting particulars of this journey were told by Miss Gardiner to Col. Lee. Arriving at the Mission on the St. Peter's river, near Lac-qui-parle lake, in the evening, she remained here one and a half days, and shifted her Indian dress, using the more becoming clothes furnished at the mission. Three days further drive, brought her to Travers, on the St. Peter's river, where the party embarked on a boat for St. Paul. On reaching Shackopee, 22d June, a crowd gathered on the landing as the boat touched; so great was the sympathy felt for her, that a sheriff raised a purse of thirty dollars immediately, and handed it to her. On the afternoon of the day of this occurrence, she landed at St. Paul. From the Agency, Miss Gardiner was brought to St. Paul, in company with Mr. Robinson and the Interpreter, together with the three Indians.

"The three Indians sent out by Maj. Flandrau, acted throughout with great bravery and discretion. They are middle-aged and intelligent looking men, and far better specimens of intelligent manhood than the average of our Indians. MA-ZA-IN-TE-MANI, who acted somewhat in the capacity of the leader of the expedition, is a Christian Indian, and is President of Dr. Riggs' Hazlewood Republic. He is noted not only as a brave and good man, but as possessing those oratorical powers for which many of the old braves are celebrated. Ink-pa-du-ta's band it is thought, crossed the Missouri, in order to effect a union with the Cheyennes, a western tribe, against whom an expedition has recently been dispatched from Fort Leavenworth. The Chayennes occupy a position of open hostility to the Government, and they seem to be the only Indians among whom Ink-pa-du-ta's band could find refuge or protection.

Miss Gardiner is now at the Fuller House. A very liberal sum of money has already been subscribed, and it will be increased. We understand it to be the intention of some philanthropic individuals to place her in a seminary where she will receive a finished education. In consideration of her past sufferings, this would seem to be, not only benevolent but just.

INTERVIEW WITH THE GOVERNOR.

At ten o'clock Tuesday morning, the three Indians who ransomed Miss Gardiner, had an interview with Governor Medary, agent Flandrau, and superintendent Cullens at the rooms of the Governor in the Fuller House, for the purpose of formally delivering over to these persons, MISS GARDINER. There were a number of ladies and gentlemen assembled in the Governor's room to witness the ceremony,—(among these was Col. L. P. LEE, of New Britain, Conn., by whom all the materials for this narrative have been furnished to the writer.)

After the Indians had shaken hands with the Governor, MA-ZA-IN-TE-MANI addressed him as follows:

"*Father*.—We have come to the white settlement, not on our own accord, but at the wish of the white people—our Father sent us off on business; we have got through with that business, and have come to meet him here.

"The American people are a great people—a strong nation; and if they wanted to, could kill all our people, but they had better judgment, and permitted the Indians to go themselves and hunt up the poor girl who was with the bad Indians. We believed when we left our kindred and friends that we would be killed ourselves; but notwithstanding this we desired to show our love to the white people. Our Father could have sent troops after Ink-pa-du-ta's band, but that would have created trouble and many innocent people would have been killed. That is the reason we desired to go ourselves. We have been among the white people a good deal, and have been assured by good traders, that the whites would always punish those who had done wrong. Last spring we heard of the troubles about Manksto, and we were very desirous to get among the Indians before the troops in order that innocent blood might not be shed.

"The WA-PE-TONS and SIS-SE-TONS made a treaty with the whites, but we are fearful even they will get into trouble. There are good and bad men everywhere—could not point to any nation where all were good. Among the CHIP-PE-WAS, the Sioux of Missouri, and the red half breeds there were good and bad men. The WA-PE-TONS and SIS-SE-TONS had sold their lands to the Great Father; he had pity on them and gave them a reserve here to live upon; but they were not well treated always. Indians had dark skin, but yet had five fingers and two eyes, and therefore wanted to be as much respected as the whites. We want to become as industrious, and as able to do something for ourselves as the whites are. We have a church, and I attend it every Sunday and hear good advice. We want good counsel; there were bad Indians, but we desired to behave well. We want this known and considered by our Great Father in Washington. The whites told us to stop making war and lay down the tomahawk. The advice was good, and we have followed it, and now our women can plant in peace. We wish to say a word in reference to the Yanktons. For many years they have had trouble with the Red River half-breeds. We told them not to fight the Red River men, as they counted themselves as Americans, and they promised us they would not. The Yanktons desired their Father should be informed of their determination, and that the Red River men should also be made acquainted with their desire for peace.

" Our Father, the Agent, desired us to go out and hunt this poor girl. The Great Spirit had pity on her and we succeeded in finding her. You see the girl here in the power of the white people. We have acted according to the will of the Agent. We now give her up to you, but desire to shake hands with her before leaving."

The above speech was addressed to Gov. Medary. Upon its conclusion, agent Flandrau desired one of the Indians present to give an account of the journey from the Yellow Medicine Agency to the camp of the Yanktons, where Miss Gardiner was discovered.

Ho-ton-wash-te, or Beautiful Voice.
From a Daguerreotype taken at St. Paul's, January 23d, 1857.

In accordance with the request, HO-TON-WASH-TE, or Beautiful Voice addressed the Agent as follows:

"*Father.*—About planting time you came up, and we started for Ink-pa-du-ta's lodges. Had we not set out then we would have had a great yield. Four days after we left Yellow Medicine, we came to the place where the other woman was killed. We took blankets, wrapped her in them and buried her. In two days more we got to the camp of the Yanktons, but Ink-pa-du-ta had got there two days before us. When we arrived, we offered every thing we had for the girl, but the Yanktons refused the first time. We waited four days and the Yanktons were divided into two parties— one desired to take her to Missouri and surrender her to the military, and others desired to bring her here. They were about quarreling when the braves determined to surrender her to us. We slept six nights before we reached the Yellow Medicine. We found you was not there and we followed you to St. Paul. The girl is yours now. Our conduct shows the heart of the Indian towards the whites. We threw away our lives to benefit the whites, in Ink-pa-du-ta's camp; but the Great Spirit had pity on us and preserved us. It shows that the Wapetons are good people. First, two men were sent out, and they brought in one of the captives, (Mrs. Marble,) and other three were sent out who also brought in one."

Mr. Flandrau addressed the Indians in response. He referred to the excitement that prevailed among the whites in consequence of the Spirit Lake Massacre, and to the fact that it was laid to the door of the entire Sioux nation. It was for this reason, and because he knew the Sioux were loyal and brave, that he asked them to volunteer and go in search of the unfortunate captives, in order that they might establish the fact that they were friendly to the whites, by rendering important services. He knew the Sioux so well that he was satisfied there would be no difficulty in procuring volunteers. He knew the expedition would succeed and had always so predicted to the whites. Mr. Flandrau concluded his remarks by addressing the Indians as follows:

"You have gone out and done your duty well and nobly; and are entitled to the gratitude of the white people. I am glad you came down here because it gave you an opportunity of seeing the Father of all the whites in the Territory and to assure him of your love to the whites. For the services you have rendered, you will be rewarded to your entire satisfaction. Your Father will start immediately on a journey to Washington, where he will see your Great Father, and be enabled to explain your part in these matters personally to him."

Governor Medary then addressed the Indians as follows:

"*My Red Children:* I am happy to meet you here because you have been performing a worthy and humane act. You have brought us back this young white girl, who was taken by those whose conduct you disapprove of. We shall endeavor to restore her to the few friends and relatives she has left, for a greater portion of them have been killed. As you have nobly and promptly risked your lives in behalf of this white woman, we hope all good whites will be as ready to succor your friends in their hour of need. I hope that the occasion will result in a renewal of the friendship of whites and Indians and that it will always be kept alive. I well understood and appreciated the danger of sending a large body of soldiers unacquainted with your country, to attempt the rescue of the women taken prisoners. There was danger that friendly Indians would be killed; and that in the end more harm would result even to the captives from such interference. I felt that Ink-pa-du-ta and his band should be punished for their crimes; but I believed and events have shown, that it was better, in order to rescue the women, to send you out. Major Flandrau and yourselves deserve the thanks of the people of Minnesota, and of the entire country, for your prompt, humane and wise action. Had any other course been adopted, the lives of many whites and friendly Indians would have been sacrificed, without the accomplishment of so much good.

"I hope the friendly Indians will hold no communication whatever with Ink-pa-du-ta's band; they are villains and murderers; and by holding communication with them, you would get yourselves into trouble with the whites. I hope there will be a lasting peace between the Indians and their white brethren in Minnesota.

"I will convey to the Great Father at Washington, an account of the good deeds you have performed, and will urge in behalf of the whites of this Territory, that all engagements entered into with you shall be faithfully carried out. I will say to him, that you desire to keep peace, and that it is the desire of the Indians adjoining you, the Yanktons, that peace should be made between them and the Red River Half Breeds, and harmony, and peace and industry restored along the borders of our Territory. These things I will convey to the Great Father. We thank you for restoring this white woman to us; and if ever Red men, women or children should be placed in such an unfortunate position, we hope to be able to treat them with equal humanity and kindness. In the name of humanity, of Christianity, and of that church you say you attend, and those precepts and counsels you heed, I again return you our thanks. We will take her, and see that you are liberally rewarded for all the trouble and danger you have subjected yourselves to in serving us."

The remarks of the Governor and the Agent were received by the Indians with their customary gravity and decorum. The usual "ho" was the only expression elicited during the speeches.

INDIAN WAR-CAP.
From a Daguerreotype taken at Dubuque, January 25th, 1857.

At the conclusion of Gov. Medary's remarks, Mr. Flandrau presented a beautiful Indian war-cap to Miss Gardiner, on behalf of MA-TO-WA-KEN, the leading Yankton chief, who desired the Indians sent in search of Miss Gardiner to present the cap to her, immediately upon their arrival into the presence of their white Father. The cap (W'mdi-wapha-the Eagle-cap) is composed of thirty-two eagle feathers, which indicate the number of scalps taken by its possessor. It is considered a mark of great honor among the Indians, the possession of such head-gear, and it entitles its proprietor to a position in the "war-path" not at all compatible with a due regard to personal safety. If the wearer exhibits in the least degree, however, the white feather, his life is forfeited. MA-TO-WA-KEN desired that it should be presented to Miss Gardiner, as a mark of his love for the whites, peaceable disposition, &c. After some little conversation in reference to the payment to be awarded to the Indians for their labor in rescuing Miss Gardiner, the council was broken up, and the Indians retired, after bidding Miss Gardiner farewell. Miss G. manifested considerable emotion during the interview, and at different periods during the speeches of the Indians, was affected to tears.

PAYMENT OF THE RANSOM.

At two o'clock on Tuesday (June 23d, 1857,) the Indians, with the Interpreter and Agent again assembled in Governor Medary's room. The sum of twelve hundred dollars was paid to the three Indians as a remuneration for their services in effecting Miss Gardiner's release. The outfit of the Indians when they started on the expedition cost about six hundred dollars. Over three thousand dollars has been expended, we believe, under the Governor's direction in securing the release of Miss Gardiner and Mrs. Marble. The Indians accompanied by their Agent and Interpreter, left the next evening (24th,) for the Agency on the Frank Steele. Superintendent Cullen also went up to attend the Sioux payment.

THE PUNISHMENT OF INK-PA-DU-TA'S BAND.

We feel authorized in announcing that measures have been adopted by Gov. Medary which will result in the extermination of Ink-pa-du-ta's band, within a very few months. Now that there are no white women in the camp of the outlaws, the Governor can prosecute his plans with that energy which will secure the speedy extermination of these women murderers. The wisdom of Governor Medary's policy has been demonstrated by the rescue of the white women alive. This is sufficient to secure him the confidence and respect of the people of Minnesota despite the caveling of fanatics, the wordy jargon of fools.

CHAPTER XIII.

"If misfortune comes she brings along the bravest virtues."—Thompson.

On Wednesday, 24th June, on board the steamer Galena, Miss Gardiner embarked in company of Gov. Medary and Col. Lee, for Dubuque, Iowa, on her way in search of her only remaining relative, her sister Eliza, who, (it will be remembered,) was absent near Fort Dodge, at the time of the massacre, and thus escaped. On parting with his young and interesting charge, the Governor was so touched with her subdued grief, and the intolerable trials she had so meekly and patiently borne, that his eyes filled with tears, in which others present joined, showing much sympathy and feeling for her:

> "No radiant pearls, which crested Fortune wears,
> No gem that twinkling hangs from Beauty's ears;
> Not the bright stars, which Night's blue arch adorn;
> Nor radiant Sun, that gilds the vernal Morn;
> Shines with such luster as the tear that flows,
> Down virtues manly cheek for others' woes."

Colonel Lee, at the request of the Governor, very gladly undertook the escort of the released captive from Dubuque to Fort Dodge. The Governor's parting charge was that if her only surviving sister could not be found, and no other provision made for her, that Col. Lee should take her to Columbus, O., where the Governor's family reside, and commit her to the care of Mrs. Medary, who would adopt her and educate her as her own. Through this whole affair, the Governor acted with a manliness and discretion, as rare as they are admirable.

During this agreeable trip, Col. Lee enjoyed the interesting society of Miss Gardiner for eight days before arriving at Fort Dodge. First to him of all the whites she had seen since her release, she told all the details of her wonderful adventures, as they have been narrated in these pages.

While in Dubuque, they had been entertained very hospitably by a private family, where an intelligent and well-educated young lady was visiting; she kindly wrote out for Col. Lee, the following description of Miss Gardiner, as she appeared at that time: "For a girl of her years, Miss Gardiner is rather tall and slender, though with a look of health and endurance. Her manners are quiet and pleasing, and her face, though so deeply browned from her long continued exposure, has a subdued and pensive expression, sufficiently attesting the suffering she has passed through. She has evidently great amiability of disposition, and to this she doubtless owes not only her life, but her exemption from many of the cruelties to which Mrs. Noble and those who evinced more spirit, were constantly subjected. She seems even now, to entertain no feelings of wrong, but only of deep thankfulness that she has been rescued from that bondage, in which she had looked forward to death as the only release, and as we might suppose, longed for its coming. She speaks of her own suffering with a calmness amounting to indifference, when compared with the depth of feeling she evinces when the dreadful fate of her family is alluded to, and it is then her woman's heart is more manifest, than in speaking of any personal abuse she has received. Her complexion is naturally light, with soft blue eyes, and brown hair. But the barbarous manner in which the squaws were accustomed to dressing it, was, in accordance with our ideas, neither of cleanliness nor beauty. They bestowed an abundance of oil from any animal they happened to have killed, and then braided it closely, allowing it to remain for days in this filthy condition, with the full force of the sun's rays burning it into her head, for she wore no protection over her head during the whole of her wanderings."

On arriving at Fort Dodge, with his ward, Col. Lee left her under the care of Major W. Williams. The Major promised to provide her as early a passage as possible to her sister when found. In St. Paul, Miss Gardiner had heard a rumor that her sister had married, and had sent messengers to Minnesota to seek for her. But not till after her arrival at Fort Dodge, could she learn where her sister had settled, nor whom she had married. After leaving her with Major Williams, in Fort Dodge, Col. Lee learned at Iowa Falls, on his return toward Dubuque, that the object of their search, (Miss Abigail's sister,) had married Mr. Wilson, and was living at Hampton, in Franklin county, Iowa. The Colonel immediately wrote to Major Williams and also to Mr. Wilson, informing the latter of Miss Gardiner's release and stay at Fort Dodge, and the former, of his discovery.

It is determined by her friends that Miss Gardiner shall be liberally educated in some proper Seminary, and one object in this publication is to aid in that most laudable determination.

> In active health or sad disease,
> O ne'er forget that precious word—
> "He shall be kept in perfect peace,
> Whose soul is stayed on God."

CHAPTER XIV.

> "So sure the fall of greatness raised on crimes!
> So fixed the justice of all-conscious Heaven!
> When haughty guilt exalts with impious joy,
> Mistake shall blast, or accident destroy;
> Weak man with erring rage may throw the dart,
> But Heaven shall guide it to the guilty heart."—*Dr. Johnson.*

MEANTIME, the savage son of Ink-pa-du-ta, who murdered Mrs. Noble, as narrated above, for want of excitement perhaps, or from better motive, turned his attention to the tender attractions of love. From this circumstance, we may judge that not all his soul was totally corrupt, that is, provided the doctrine of Charles Lamb,

> "Man while he loves is not quite depraved,"

applies to Indians as well as whites. A maiden of the Annuity Indians was the happy possessor of his heart, such as it was, and accepted his invitation to become his bride. While on a journey in the charming month of June, to visit his father-in-law, about the time that their honey moon was in its zenith, and as subsequent events show, was about to wane, never to wax again, he and his lovely squaw lodged one night in a small Indian village, about five miles from the Yellow Medicine Agency.

What must have been his horror, when looking out from his lodge on the morning of the 1st of July, 1857, his eye caught sight of Major Flandrau and one of the three Indians who had ransomed Miss Gardiner. In an instant, his bloody murder of Mrs. Noble, and all his other diabolical acts, must have flashed on his mind, in all their ghastliness, threatening at last, the VENGEANCE he justly feared and so richly deserved! Seizing his gun he rushed from the lodge in the vain effort to escape his pursuer:

> "Over rock and over" meadow,
> "Through brush and brake and forest,

> Ran the guilty Ink-pa-du-ta;
> "Like an antelope he bounded,
> Till he came unto a hollow
> In the middle of the " prairie;
> Then in rapid chase departed
> His pursuers white and sable,
> "On the trail of" Ink-pa-du-ta,
> "Through the forest where he passed it,
> To the headlands where he rested,"
> And "they found" him Ink-pa-du-ta,
> Hiding in the "trampled grapes"
> In the hollow of the prairie,
> "Found the couch where he" was resting,
> When he thought to hide his "body."

Major Flandrau had with him several soldiers and friendly Indians, who immediately on reaching the ravine where skulked the doomed fugitive, fired and severely wounded him. The Indian returned their attack by shooting with his double-barreled gun, and one of his charges struck the cartridge box of a soldier. Enraged by this, the soldier rushed forward and impaled the bleeding savage on his bayonet! Several wounds were counted in the carcase of the now lifeless murderer, who was left, as the body of Mrs. Noble had been left by him, lying on the ground. His pursuers having secured the widowed squaw, returned to the Agency.

Major Flandrau had heard on the 20th of June, that three Indians of Ink-pa-du-ta's band were lurking near the Agency, and immediately dispatched a trusty Indian to spy their whereabouts. His plans were secretly and skillfully laid. With a detachment from company D, 10th Infantry, from Fort Ridgeley, under command of Lieut. Murray, he himself led on the pursuers, accompanied by faithful Indians, on the 1st July. HO-TON-WASH-TE, or Beautiful Voice, one of the three who rescued Miss Gardiner at the risk of their lives, was one of the party.

The two companions of the son of Ink-pa-du-ta, were thought to have fled to Skunk Lake, to the camp of their old chief, and fears were rife that they would revenge, by new cruelties on innocent settlers, the blood of their fallen young leader.

In a letter dated Sioux Agency, July 3d, 1857, Major Flandrau writes as follows, after describing the execution:

"On our way from the place where we had killed the Indian, we passed through a large camp, and met them all naked, painted and armed, ready to give fight. They, however, did not fire, and we passed on.

MALEDICTION.

"I never saw so much bustle and excitement among the Indians as the next three hours presented. They assembled at the house where we were, about three hundred strong, all armed and naked, but made no positive demonstration. That night we armed all the men we could, and passed the whole night awaiting an attack.

"The Indians brought up the body, and had a large and long council over it; and many speeches were made, similar in their objects to that of Anthony over the body of Cæsar; but they did not find a response sufficient to induce an attack.

"The next morning we left for this Agency, and are awaiting the arrival of Sherman's battery, which reached Fort Ridgeley to night. I have about fifty men under arms, with Charley Jenney and Mr. Morse, who are on a visit here, acting as Lieutenants. Everything is quiet, but prudence is always best in these cases.

"Yours,
"C. E. FLANDRAU."

The Indians around the Agency seemed very much excited and displeased with the summary punishment of young Ink-pa-du-ta, and particularly that his squaw was taken to the Agency. She was released immediately, however, when the Agent knew that she was innocent of the crimes of Ink-pa-du-ta's band. Her release seemed to appease the Indians. We confess that the writing of this last chapter has cost us less sympathy and pain than that of any other in this book wherein deaths are described. We only hope that the satisfaction of the reader in the justice meted out to young Ink-pa-du-ta, may equal the pain of reading the above details of murder and wrong. And I am sure I can rely on a mental "amen" from every reader, to the wish, *So may perish all the foul participators in the fiendish crimes of Ink-pa-du-ta's band!*

> "Not so long and wide the world is,
> Not so rude and rough the way is,
> But that wrath shall overtake" them
> And dread "vengeance may attain" them!"

APPENDIX.

From the Fort Dodge Sentinel, July 30th, 1857.

FOUND.—The remains of two human bodies were found, one day last week, in the neighborhood of Little Sioux River, and from the marks about them, are supposed to be the remains of Messrs. Burckholder and Johnson; they were members of the Spirit Lake expedition, and were lost on their way home. Some of our citizens have started for Little Sioux for the remains, intending to bring them to this place for identification. They will probably return by Sunday afternoon. The commander of the expedition has issued orders for companies A, B and C, to meet on Sunday and act as an escort to the last remains of their former companions.

TO THE MEMBERS OF COMPANIES A, B AND C, OF THE SPIRIT LAKE EXPEDITION:—You are requested to meet at the Treasurer and Recorder's office, on Sunday afternoon, (August 2d,) to take charge of the remains of your late comrades, Burckholder and Johnson, who are supposed to be found, and whose remains will be here on that day.

EXCITEMENT AT SPIRIT LAKE.—We have noticed of late that fears are entertained of the safety of the Spirit Lake settlement, and we are inclined to the opinion that such fears are well-founded. Indeed, we suppose the danger to be apprehended from the Sioux and other Indian tribes, will be more imminent and extensive, than is at present anticipated. The death of the son of Ink-pa-du-ta, has aroused a spirit of hostility and revenge, and the refusal of the Government in paying over the annuity, has added to the cause of the dangers now anticipated. Within a few days, several of the settlers from Spirit Lake have reached our place. They report that two scouts from Red Wing reached Spirit Lake, advising the settlers that a band of the Sioux and Yanktons, numbering about five hundred, were up in arms and threatened the destruction of all the settlements on the upper Des Moines. They report that the Lake settlement will be immediately abandoned.

We are not aware what arrangements have been made by the Governor of Minnesota to avert the danger, but the probability is, a sufficient government force will be put into the field to check the progress of the savage tribes. We shall expect by our next issue to have some definite information on the subject.

From the Red Wing Gazette.

FROM SPIRIT LAKE.—Our fellow-citizen, Mr. John Day, recently returned from the scene of the tragedy at Spirit Lake, has given us a partial statement thereof. It seems that cold-blooded brutality and heartlessness, is not confined to the savages.

The case he mentions is of a person who soon after the massacre, took possession, in other words, "jumped" the claim of Mr. Gardiner, whose daughter was captured by the savages. On the claim was a good log-house, (into which he moved,) furniture, &c. A few rods in front of the house, Mr. Gardiner and his family, in all, nine persons, had been buried in one grave, with temporary head and foot stones erected to mark the spot. This person, to obliterate all traces of the former owner, enclosed the grave with his field, and drove the plow over it in connexion with the rest of the field.

No further comment is necessary; a deed more atrocious or heartless, was never committed by the most blood-thirsty savage. His name is Prescott. His profession—a minister of the gospel, one of the thousand other scoundrels who were writing such heart-rending stories from Kansas, of the outrages committed upon themselves and neighbors by the border ruffians.

Prescott started for Sioux City before Mr. Day left, to purchase Half Breed script to locate upon this claim. Mr. Day is of the opinion that the Rev. gentleman will find Spirit Lake a more "outrageous" country than Kansas. We hope Miss Gardiner's rights will be looked after in this case.

Mr. Day reports further robberies lately committed by annuity Indians; two houses were plundered of all their contents. Luckily, the owners were not at home.

www.ingramcontent.com/pod-product-compliance
Lightning Source LLC
Chambersburg PA
CBHW061516040426
42450CB00008B/1640